THE DEVIL'S GARDEN

The Devil's Garden

Adrian Matejka

Alice James Books

FARMINGTON, MAINE

10 9 8 7 6 5 4 3 2 1

Alice James Books are published by Alice James Poetry Cooperative, Inc., an affiliate of the University of Maine at Farmington.

ALICE JAMES BOOKS
238 MAIN STREET
FARMINGTON, ME 04938
www.alicejamesbooks.org

LIBRARY OF CONGRESS CATALOGING-IN-PUBLICATION DATA
Matejka, Adrian, 1971–
The devil's garden / Adrian Matejka.
    p. cm.
ISBN 1-882295-41-2
1. Racially mixed people—Poetry. 2. Indians of North America—Poetry.
3. African Americans—Poetry. I. Title.
PS3613.A825D48 2003
    811'.6—dc21   2003008133

Alice James Book gratefully acknowledges support from the University of Maine at Farmington and the National Endowment for the Arts. ❧

COVER ART: "(And the Gods made Love . . .)" by Kevin Neireiter. Oil on canvas 8x10 inches. Reprinted courtesy of the artist.

Thank you to the editors of the following magazines where these poems first appeared, sometimes in different renditions: *Beacon Street Review:* "Integration"; *Clackamas Literary Review:* "The Devil's Garden"; *Crab Orchard Review:* "Con Leche"; *Elixir:* "English B," "Home Remedies," "The Official Story"; *goodfoot:* "Memento"; *Hooked:* "Crap Shoot," "Vinyl"; *Lake Effect:* "Peace and Soul"; *Perihelion:* "Postlude"; *Poetry Midwest:* "Klimt in Chicago," "White Pages"; *Shampoo Poetry Magazine:* "Want"; *Sou'wester:* "Conjugating Opposites," "Pigment," "To Have This," "Understanding Al Green"

Thanks to the people who helped make this thing happen: Richard Cecil, Jo Gustin, Allison Joseph, Ruth Ellen Kocher, Robert Matejka, Michael Molino, Kevin Neireiter, Sean Singer, Melanie Rack, Cedric Ross, Jon Tribble, and Daniel Wideman. Thanks also to my sisters and brothers at Cave Canem and Vermont Studio Center.

FOR EDNA

CONTENTS

3.

Man cannot express that which does not
exist—either in the form of dreams, ideas
or realities—in his own environment.

—RALPH ELLISON

Being mixed, you're the man of the future.
Too bad the future isn't now.

—RODNEY JONES

I

Autobiography as Language

Blame military life, family scuttling
from Los Angeles to Germany,

back again before my words
could find the vocal fold of English.

Blame the bilinguality of chance.
German first—ham fisted umlauts,

non-negotiable consonants stacked
by the hubbub of need. Blame

the new neighborhood, four parts
Mexican, no parts half-blood.

Or blame me, cardboard color heavier
than a sneaker in the back, fist

that makes the jaw clack. If the Mexicans
bum-rushing me before school

was bad, my mother making them
lunches was worse. *You know they*

don't have any food, pushing me out.
Peanut butter and jelly in tow for Alex,

Chucho, and John: brawlers who would
rather swing than understand why I looked

3

like them, but sounded like the man
at the newspaper stand. Blame pain,

turning everyone a ripe shade. Language
comes before crawling. Blame that.

English B

authority figure

I had to be introduced to The Man.
He was around before 1977.
I just couldn't see him, like air
or welfare. My mom told me:
No matter what you do, the Man
is going to try and keep you down.
I already knew no one was keeping
me down. So when teacher asked
me to read from *Kaleidoscopes*,
I told her *back off, white woman.*
I'm not reading your books.
She laughed, but understood
when I threw my book, covers
flapping like man's first scraps
with gravity. Teacher realized
she wasn't keeping me down,
so I got sent to Remedial English.
When I looked up "remedial,"
the dictionary read: "The Man
questioning your authenticity."
Then I looked up "authenticity."
Dictionary definition: "Blackness."
So I was authentic and The Man
could keep his remedial. Problems
began when I realized my mom
was The Man, too: five feet
two inches, curling red afro,
white with power fist
in the air. Half-black, half-white
boy sitting on the stoop,
counting pieces of glass,
trying not to keep himself down.

5

Want

Bass lines like fat men squeezing into
3rd grade desks.

Coltrane's squealing right before I was born.

If not,
        a pill that makes
the music in my head stop.

Immediately, then I won't know
what I'm missing.

I want dissimilar words, hyphenated
by minty-fresh breath. What good
are words
        if no one will listen?

A way-back machine, so I can fix.

        William Shatner, circa 1967:
guest host for my 8th birthday party.

I'm wishing for mandibles, clipping
the staccato lilt.

Mandibles for tailoring a new dress.
My woman needs one.

Then, X-ray vision,
        so I can ignore
        what I wish for.

I want irrefutable skin
like Luke Cage, Hero for Hire.

In the semi-embarrassment of silence,
I want to understand

why Goya used spoons to paint
                instead of leaves.

                If nothing else—
a map with the exact location

of the crossroads, so I can believe
what I never should have known.

Crap Shoot

Three of us, in a circle, shooting
craps. Instead of crumpled bills
or food stamps, we used an army man,

a Dukes of Hazzard matchbox car
and Coca-Cola bottle caps, all
with "C" underneath. Never the "L"

that would have won us a million,
that hook of phonics keeping
my friends from seeing Mo run

from the apartment next to us.
But they saw White Boy come
after, shotgun in the crook bursting

the door like Superman, wood
and hinges flying like a drunk dad after
kids. They saw him aim that shotgun,

catch Mo's back with two. They saw
that man break apart on the pavement
like a carton of milk. White Boy: *Bring*

back my shit, muthafucka and Mom
dragging me inside, her sweating
fingers braceleted around my wrist.

Paris, Texas (1954)

White faces spring
                from the crowd:
dandelions in the front lawn.

Ropes so tight I can
feel flies prowl fibers.
Their legs, a twisting frenzy.

Police uniforms in flies'
                eyes, floating like fish
breath from the river's

bottom, so I stay down,
                crumbs. Someone near

hawks soda and beer
to white people splitting ribs,
                arms against the platform's

splintering wood.
Nose mashed into lip,
                unforgiving as the sticks

and fists spilling
                over my face. *You
                won't be touching
                another white woman.*

A dirty child, dirty yellow hair,
perched on father's shoulders.

9

She licks a cone wet
            with sugar diamonds,
ice cream dripping
father's shirt sleeve.

Let me have five
minutes with that black
son of a bitch.
                  Re-routed trains
bloating the sweaty crowd.

Some woman curses my ape
mother. Sheriff pulls a knife.

He cuts my arm.
My skin,
            the slow fire

around the break. My arm.

The hangman:
Nigger, you gonna die slow.

The man cuts my chest.

My heart beating,
                  hanging outside.
He starts sawing.

Pieces of skin in strips like bacon.

To Have This

1. My Story:

Dad moved out after Mom cut
her hand on ice. I helped
cram all he owned into the car:
records and records in milk crates—
Bitches Brew, brown faces crowding
the back window. Fatigues, boots
shiny and black like the drill sergeant
sunglasses hiding his eyes. I went
to give him five (*All the cats do it
like this*. Hands brush, then point
the index finger) but he hugged me.
I pulled away, looked to see
if my friends saw. He reached into
the trunk, pulled out a mirror: *I want
you to have this so you will always
know how good we look*. He was gone,
and I looked into my mirror, saw
Afro Sheen prints lining the edges
of the wood frame. All pointing at me.

2. Mother's Story:

I told the neighbors
I slipped on a patch
of ice, but my hand

is still outlined
by Agent Orange,
straight from Dak To

to our Frankfurt apartment.
That night, I found him
in the hallway, naked.

Bowie knife trailing
along the plaster. He cut
tunnels in the white walls

beneath an oil painting
of mountains. He said:
I've got to get them

while they are asleep.
I reached for him.
A quick stab, the wall

sprinkled with my blood.
I fell and he ran
out the door, into

frozen Frankfurt night.
His mouth in a scream,
but no sound.

The History of Bad Luck

The first time I heard an owl,
Edna told me those disgruntled
echoes bring all misfortune
in Mexico: lost teeth, lost lighter,
lost way. Where I come from
that's called blues—bad luck
revolves around who you borrow
money from, how soon they come
looking. Your neighbors taking
inventory while you're moving in.
Flat tires and hair loss aren't bad luck.
Catching your woman necking
in a parking lot is. Owls have little
to do with gun shots or beat-downs;
they straddle a line between blue
and uncomfortability. The day before
I met Edna's parents, this owl
foretold a new blues: her retired
vaquero of a father working on
the car—Maglite in one hand,
biggest wrench in the world
in the other—me standing there,
gift bottle of tequila slack
like extra rope for the hangman,
owl-shaped target on my cranium.

The Devil's Garden

The first missionary traveling through,
God-driven mission hampered by blisters:
Such a forlorn place must surely be

the Devil's garden. Since he was in
a hurry to leave, the name stuck.
By that time, volcanoes compacted

trees, turned soil into a crust so thick
only brambles try rooting. Lightning
as fractional as sign language split

trunks into stone thighs. Rain shaped ribs
in the branches. Nothing resembling
a heart in between, unless it was

the sun, honeycomb of rise and set making
crows tap-dance landscapes more lunar
than anything else. The crows say the universe

is expanding. With it, Earth, the missionary,
his unsaved savages, woebegotten belly
songs. Through it all, the Garden settles

itself, snug in solitary geology. The Devil,
he's got free reign, surrounded by rocks
so sharp they work like spit before a curse.

No more missionaries—only tourists,
and flies and the flies' shadows, relaxed,
with no particular place to be.

The Meaning of Rpms

Pearl, blind and jobless, employed
me: hours of switching records
while friends played basketball out back.
Clang of ball on rim, somebody yelling
Brick! Shuffle of chain nets antsy
like the last school bell. Each meeting
of metal and rubber accentuating
Cannonball's solos as if he'd pushed
all 250 of his pounds into
that childish horn. I put up with it all.
Not because I liked her, but for the buck
she paid me. Before I learned sympathy,
blindness meant lamps on day and night.
Or being able to make clown faces
and not get into trouble, even though Pearl
wasn't born blind. A cook, she found
herself putting cinnamon where paprika
was needed. Baking soda instead of flour.
Even in the kitchen's halogen,
ingredients became dark, granular.
Nothing. The dishwasher ratted when
he caught Pearl tasting: nutmeg, breath
of too-cold air. Flour like a mouth
too tired to run anymore. She never
talked about cooking. Only the music
I said I liked. But Pearl could tell
I was lying just by hearing me talk.

Ode to Eddie Hazel

(1950-1992)

1.

It's not the circumference of brim
that matters,
        or the evolution of feathers

keeping time from velvet wraparound.

But the skull,
the skull and hands. Dismantling lips,
mad dash tongue.
                Accentuating licks

from a fish-hooked body
preened by strings, cat-gut
                or otherwise.

2.

Good Thoughts, Bad Thoughts:

Guitar gathering anti-matter
beside stars—street lamps through
                9-volt socket—
                not seen with undressed eye.

Dissecting the top from the black
beneath sneakers' squeak.

Reflection of bus chrome,
refracted out
of ligament, city dust.

Song-singing sliver between shirt
and skirt freewheeling
all the way down the knees
way down the knees

left brain juke-bent ego plugged.
Signifying woman tone.

Lullaby for a junkie's coffle.

Obligatory Mingus

That same hi-yella misfit passing
as Mexican. Conk not style. Necessity.
There is no love in being neither
here nor there. Bellow of a man,
stark in January's embalmed sun.
Let My Children Hear Music means
something else. Surrounded
by eight-year-olds, open as go-go
dancers who thought he wouldn't
dare. He did. Overcoat slumped
on seesaw, white underwear discarded
on a bush. Fistful of C notes
decrescendoing, almost worth
their weight in fig leaves. That same:
strangely compliant, swamped
by confused children as whitecoats
led him away, underdog no more.

Earth Will Seduce You

The secular nature of
skin, uneven embouchure

of lips rubbing. Slow yawn
signifying leaving as

the last great asterisk. Hands
lose firmness, but lips remain.

Ruffle of hip unsettled
by skirt: cloth and noise, until

Sidney Bechet's clarinet
is all the good ears can do.

Acupuncture for tongue,
unexpected like fish scales

ground in lipstick. But it's there,
phenomena retailed as if

memory is inside rather
than out. Mirage of compression,

those lips. Closest I've been
to dying was a sneeze. All

functioning stopped: no bassed-up
heart, liver tremolo. Stopped,

but not easily like sheet music.
Understand Sidney Bechet

downed a man over chord changes.

Her Gardens

. . .were the gardens I spoke of
when I spoke to you of gardens.
—Michael Ondaatje

At night, she comes to me, a gospel torn
from buckets full of skin and hair. This night,
inside my distended head, she is calm,

peeling orange rinds. The peels warn
of madness pressed into citrus, the fight
for juice and pith. Her patience is a Psalm

in movement. I run my finger along
the creases in her palm. A stalagmite
of orange rind reminds me that I suspend

her progress. Oranges always invite
elevation: they are the fruit borne
in harvest moons, dream glances. I pretend
not to see her looking, but I intend
to take Michelle to my lips like a horn.

2

Pigment

Blue

They say the Devil owns all blues,
transcendental dream-shaded: indigo

heavier than cat-gut when the moon
is preening. Cobalt homespun in Zaire,

the country itself an outline of monopoly,
lacking palate. Belly-color blue.

They say Picasso played the Devil's
game because he couldn't afford red

paint. My woman's slept-in hair
can be blue. Mid-squawk vocal chord,

taffeta ghost in a devil's chorus. Call blue
I don't know why like the weight of water.

Red

Monk's forgotten triangles of color. Leftover stew meat
in the fold, shouldn't have been seen red. Down the drain,
armatured memory. Brewed melanin red. My brother's

5th grade handwriting, slide of needle punctuation. Need
the pop for cursive, like red-branched trees applauding wind
just because. Red is the color of nausea, serration of tongue

and lung intersection. Panhandling Eddie Hazel: eyes
like Romare Bearden's color on a good day. Misnomer red,
an apostrophe of ash trying to separate tobacco from bone.

Ochre

It's in the rise of skirt
around thighs. Not seeing
makes the difference.
Haves and nots falling apart,
molecules at a time,
and there's nothing
to be done, no paint to fill
spaces. Memory's
predication: ring in belly,
garters reaching hips,
meniscus of silk between
arched middles. God's
ignored love songs: O,
serenity of orange.
None of Goya's witches.
Just porcelain curve
split by gravity's symmetry,
the natural way of evening
out space stereophonically.
Dusty orange, running hips
like a drowned man
still scrimping sand.

Black, White

Ecology leads to mulattoed color,
lulled by ambiguity's generosity.
That husk of absorbed light,
those slim-spired Gaudí concoctions.
Check the cortex for totality in colors,
black. Or find flesh stripped for
Siqueiros' brick underside: white.
Check the rinds for permutations.
Sienna, teal, or magenta—
improvisation in a modal spectrum.

Conjugating Opposites

Body: mismanaged carapace
of *was*. You'd be better
as constellation, ignoring light
years of interstellar bric-a-brac.
You could be *Hammer Muted
by Shirt Sleeve* or *Sleep*

Trip-Wired with Trumpets.
If I could remake you, I'd shape
the maker's image. Adam's
apple like a fistful of Tuesdays.
No more chin music. Once
new eyes adjusted, you'd see

only teal. A modernistic world
near-spun in blue, air and water
conjugate afterthoughts of Earth.
The trick: understanding vibrato
waking you nights when noise
and nights are anachronistic space.

The Official Story

I stopped claiming Indian blood
when the government told me:
no proof. Grandma, full-blooded
Delaware orphan adopted
by Black farmers trying to save
her. New daughter in tow,
the family headed straight for
the tribal headquarters to make
her Black: crossing out names,
birth certificate burned. Shredding
any and all pictures of her
as Indian, screwdriver scratching
her from the tribal monument,
because disproof isn't proof
and erasure means forgetting.
Genetics are all they left—
half-breed son of a different half
dusted with disco, Afro Sheen
instead of war paint. A half-half
breed grandson, still not
finding his name on the ledger.

Me in *The Garden of Music*

Fields of pigment
      in a painter's head,
      but empty of tomatoes

or green beans. Skin,
canvas: browns, blacks,

primitive maroon
      leaving no room for
      wrinkles or cirrhosis.

Here, prejudice revolves
around timbre and improv.

We are all seamless:
      Ornette, the center—
      horn stunted (*New York*

is Now! but not right now)
because Ed Blackwell plays

a left-lobe migraine,
      drum speaking biblically
      and Coltrane whets

the saxophone first
(as if *Sunship* introduced

understanding to humans).
      Oblivious to colors,
      Coltrane tastes all

sounds inherent in Genesis.
Genealogy: squawk-filled

joints limbered in darker
  tones and definition
  is simply more paint.

Bob Thompson is optic here.
In this garden, music comes

apart, ripe or not: ruminating
  horses are in key, while
  humans try to find an exit.

Ankle-Deep in Ocean

Broken jellyfish, misplaced shells
swirling: wet means something,

but has nothing to do with vegetation.
Turquoise in tight-lipped waves. Brown

eyes reflect time in water. A broken
branch elbows her, a drowned

man's arm trying to swim. Underneath,
a triangle of sea glass she tosses

away, looking for a better one. All
I have is what I can pocket. Handfuls

of beach rocks, dry as pulled molars.

Home Remedies

    —A. M. Jackson, Creal Springs, Illinois

The science of hate isn't exact.
It works, like a child making
explosives with junior chemistry.
Most times, it's voodoo: hats
on beds, mirrors backwards,
the Devil beating his wife because
the sun shines when it rains. No
fact-based explanations, but tried
and true excuses. 10 pm, serving
food at a restaurant outside
DeSoto, Illinois, and A. M. Jackson
is a geneticist. When he theorized
my neck was strong, it made sense.
He said, *I was a pro in my day.*
Maker of knot doubled tight
like a fist before it breaks a rib.
Able to utilize the crook between
trunk and limb as a pulley, to snap
a neck for maximum flopping,
man no longer a man, more
a fish that forgot what water is.

What He Wanted to Say

—after meeting Muhammad Ali, 1987

The verbal ropadope:
slow words on
a no-show tongue.

I've got a thesaurus
in my brain and washcloths
for hands.
          Don't feel
sorry—spent my life
in the kitchen with
the Devil. Spent my life
hop-scotching punches
that make a man
check his language

and seven years
can be longer
than you think when
you've got a whupping
sitting on your chest.

Preacher (1942)

With one moonshine eye,
tried focusing the back door
of Big Mike's. After midnight,
somebody wailing on a harp.
All I could do was throw up
all over a stubby bush: bits
of greens, cornbread covering
suffering leaves, the same
crustiness on the front of my shirt.
The moon, an evil wink,
and I stayed back there,
behind that shack, vomiting
like it was the last day. I fell
on hands and knees in wet
dust, prayed to God
to make it stop. But he wasn't
hearing me. I said the same thing
most nights, anyway. He wasn't
believing me. God knew my heart.
He could feel it beat faster
when a fine woman walked by,
could see it jump when I took
the night's Mason jar to my lips.
He knew Robert Johnson
was my friend, that I told him how
to make that deal. This time,
I knew I was at my low.
Robert, dead for wrongdoing,
poisoned by a red-eyed husband.
I didn't want to be like that,
any more than I wanted

to be that man out back
pissing and crying in my own vomit.
So I put my sticky hands together
right there, right behind that den
of sin, kneeling in my dinner,
and prayed that God take it
all away, that God would make me
a better man. But He didn't.

Genealogy of Insomnia

How long wilt thou sleep, O sluggard?
when wilt thou arise out of thy sleep?

—PROVERBS 6:9

1. *Sand*

Regardless, there is always
that stained-glass peacock
the ocean, reminding
we are all skeleton, the blues
a worn skin orphaning us
inside the front matter.
All bones, no scrub.

2. *Indigo Suite*

The tongueless sea,
mouth full of gravel
and bones. Saltwater release:
parchment lingering, white.
Rinsed like worked gristle.
Anticipation of another
evening trying to wake up.

3. *Etceteras*

Someplace else, this might
be called moss, but in a foreign
room, so far from any water,

it's called a bed of flesh.
Not quite sex, though it might
seem like it. Mutual signifying
without consideration of buoyancy.

4. *Perdido*

Sleep, but not weekdays,
spent clamoring against
consequence. Misery can be
a broken branch when you
don't know how to swim.
Ceaseless, to shore.
Ceaseless, to sleep.

For What It's Worth

If you send your ear
to a lover, your mouth
will be your nose's only friend.

If I sit too long,
                halogen lamps
are contrafacts of Tito Puente's
shock and buffer timbales.

Azaleas taste like words
            if you suck the pistils.

I wish someone
would upgrade the afro-pick:

                        weapon or alarm,
                remote for car and van.

A troublesome fact:
there is no
        English translation

for timbales. The word
is onomatopoeia.

I forgot where my nose is.

I wish I could meet Billie Holiday
sixty years ago when
            I learned childhood.

I wanted to be a fireman,
but they have plastic hats
     instead of guns.

I have no idea what azaleas
     look like, but they sound

like what my Native friend says
instead of "fine, thank you."

Integration

No amount of hoodoo could convince
me that anything was wrong but the music.
I remember saying: *What's wrong*

with this place? Nothing but country.
Still spinning the table-top jukebox,
even though the songs were the same

as the first time around. In Tennessee,
music travels faster than prayers
for a silent god, but no one wants

to hear Stevie Wonder. I was sure
simplicity would change Hank Williams
into Al Green; Curlee, Tennessee,

to Los Angeles. But it couldn't, any more
than music dampens the smell
of Confederate grease, what my mother

called "Southern-fried anger."
Or sweat-creased stares that had less
to do with my Black father sitting next

to her. More with me, like a blind man
eating peas with a knife. In the old days,
funnels and oil-skin sacks inside white

hoods—unfulfilled thirsts of dead
Confederate soldiers for the superstitious
here, white sheets the ghost-skin, cold

enough to make a Black man leave town
by moonlight. Me saying *This place sucks*
didn't help. My mother, dragging me

by my afro, away from the sweetest tea
I'd tasted didn't help: still no Stevie.
Only an agreed-upon silence in the diner.

Eight Positions Mistaken as Love

1. Man and woman, separated by two thousand
   miles, only what they can remember holding them
   is *quarantine.*

2. *Hibernation* can be holding hands, jellyfish rain
   coating fingers. No kissing in public.

3. Man and woman on a couch, looking conversation
   but murmuring nothing like deaf cicadas
   is called *euphonium.*

4. *Insomnia* is the muscularity of passion lost.
   It starts, he noticing the bags beneath her eyes.
   She, aware of the misdirection of his teeth.

5. *Quernicia* is a woman rubbing the smooth marrow
   of a man's palm in public when no one knows
   they are together.

6. When a man uses his tongue to check a woman's
   eye for the eyelash, it is called *sampling marmalade.*

7. A man and woman, lying down to sleep, but continuing
   to pull each other close. Turbid flesh to sinew, sinew
   to bone: *absolution.*

8. When a man and woman curve into each other, make
   a quiet topography of flesh, they become
   the *devil's apostrophe.*

3

Understanding Al Green

When I was twelve, a wiser sixteen-
year-old told me: *If you really want
to get that, homeboy, you best be bringing
Al Green's Greatest Hits. And if you ain't
in the mix by song five, either she's
dyking it or you need to re-evaluate your
sexual orientation. Know what I'm saying?*

With those words, I was off—borrowed Al
Green in the clutch in search of that *thing.*
Socks pulled up to my neck. A curl. Real
tight Hoyas jersey was nothing but regulation
and I knew I was smooth and I knew
I was going to be in the mix by song five.
The whole walk from the ball court,

the wise man's words echoed like somebody's
mama banging on the door: *the panties
just be slippin' off when the women hear
Al's voice. Slippin'.* Slippin' because Al
hits notes mellow, like the silk that silk
wears. His voice is all hardworking night time
things. Not fake breasts, but you

and your woman, squeezed onto the couch,
taking a nap while the aquarium stutters
beside you. Nodding off on drizzly days
when you should be at work. The first
smoke after a glass of fine wine you know
you can't afford. Nobody, woman
or man, knows how to handle Al Green.

That Girl from Ipanema would have
dug Al. Her panties, flip-flopping right
there by the sea. That sexy passing
the Pharcyde by would have stopped to say
What up? if they were Al. But they weren't.
And neither were you, last night when
that woman at the club shut you down:

I got a man. . .blah, blah, blah. Hate to tell you,
player, but she's at Al's place right now asking
for an autograph and maybe a little sumpin-
sumpin. What is sumpin-sumpin? I don't know.
But Al knows. And I'm sure you've heard that old
jive about Al getting scalding grits thrown on him.
You have to recognize those lies because

he would have started singing and those grits
would have been in the mix, too. For real.
I never believed the pimp-to-preacher story
anyway. The point is, Al's voice is like G-strings
and afro wigs and trying to be quiet when
the parents are home. The point is Al Green
hums better than most people dream.

Contrafact (of an Ars Poetica)

1.

Eliot was right the first time.
October is the cruelest month,

a fusion of maroon, immature
green introducing cold. October

pilfers summer from trees
and squirrels. Even words flip

the script in fall, hibernating
vowels and syllables. But at 10:30,

the train still sounds like
a devil coughing.

2.

Ashy fingers are cranky
as worn-out lips these days,

abscesses of a jive-ass pen.
Words: modal, like no-name

polish on a pawn-shop horn.
Ink makes notes and even

English sounds like music if
you make words swing

like the Devil's in the kitchen
waiting for your mama.

Betwixt and Between

Miscegenation's capitol
is the mule. Not quite horse,
almost donkey. No useful
erection to speak of.
In any unnatural concoction,
somebody's got to take
the blame. Freud would say
credit the mother if props
are necessary.
              Mulattos
are human mules—half
black, most times more
than half white—misogynous
on a good day. All the while,
impotent between tribes.
Blame: gift of the exotic,
like Hendrix opening
for the Monkees, or Othello
key-holed by Iago. Blessed
be he with the hybrid vigor
of melanin, arrested between
the sun and the sun.

To the Miscarried Child

The precipitate of Jennifer
            and me. The same day we saw

the Mariners play, sperm and egg
            rose, carbonation. The backwash:

matrix of an unformed survivor.
            My affirmation—you had her eyes.

They were lost in a cataract
            of misplaced blood. You had

my smile as if you knew what
            was happening before you looked

it up. Even though I didn't. Did you
            try and comfort her, humming

jazz riffs while she slept?
            Summer nights, I would sound

"Soleo" near her ear until
            she slept. Did you hear it?

Con Leche

If in fact, you are what you eat, I absorbed
that beating like a plateful of plantains.
Even before I made the mistake of calling

him Mexican, Hugo didn't like me. No one
in his family had a job, rent money coming
from my mom—the one white person

in that L.A. neighborhood—for baby-sitting.
Maybe it was being darker than me that pissed
him off or the way his sister said I was *muy*

guapo despite my gap-teeth, Black father. Or
because I told him only wetbacks ate rice,
and plantains tasted like fake bananas, right

after his mother served both mixed in a bowl
as breakfast again. *I'm tired of eating like
a Mexican* and I was grounded after the first

punch: heap of crying rice, milk, and those
plantains. It's tough to run, belly full of *arroz
con leche* no matter what country of origin.

Cramps from rice sponging everything in sight.
Milk belly-ache. Sore jaw from Hugo's hook,
Puerto Rican pride in a city of misnomers.

Miles Runs the Voodoo Down

Back to the crowd,
Miles hunches
against the spotlight's weight.
He is a fist
of glitter punched up
through the stage.

His horn strains
methodic notes
for the crooked-eyed
insomniacs in octaves
at his feet.

When he plays:
lily-gray smoke,
swirls of light stretching
up from his eyes. Muted
reflections in coffee cups

crumble like the discarded
orange of cigarette butts
that hit the floor as squeaking
squealing subway wheels,
metal lips shivering against
metal wheels, sparks spraying

to the sides, heating a path
on the overcoats
of businessmen, unshaven
in movie poster rows,
late for work, briefcases
filled with noise, hanging
arms numbly near the floor.

He never turns.
Only passes from the stage,
sweat trailing in sequined drops.
(Miles' voice in the background
like dry rocks: *Walk*
like that, baby.
Yeah. Walk like that.)

Insect Precipitate and Saltwater

—for Edna

The moon manifests itself still,
even on the craziest of days. Ocean,
tides folding again, as if to fill
the half-starved moon

with leftovers: pirates and sea stars. Motion,
grains of damp sand swirling, until
they hide shells with gravity's commotion.

Your hair, made from butterflies, isn't real.
Indigos and reds, an alchemist's potion.
I smooth back your hair; I mill:
butterflied halves of the broken moon.

Klimt in Chicago

On the Elevated Train

bucking past Chicago's topography:
concrete and soot, wig stores. Starter
jackets in windows, mouthless
mannequins starting nothing but trouble.
Despite the cold, horizontal stars look
closer above the metallic clang
that makes a city a city. This time,
Secession comes to the town
not from the South, but from Vienna
served on a paint palate: wild-eyed
watercolor women, oil-embalmed men
dulled by entwined shades. Half-sealed
office windows lit with oil.

Klimt's Women

Pre-dawn bruised
                by trains grumbling
like a bass with a broken string.

The women are washed
in a mezzanine of geometry.

                Chattering in paint
like a topiary outrunning itself.

Collage of stained glass
    covering the body's archeology.

Klimt knows the speed of beauty.

How it will leave you
    bed ridden with
    the memory of once.

No shadows in memory,
only paint's mute
    understanding of skin.

The difference between painter
and canvas is the in
and out of breathing.

Waterworks

Mermaids and mermaids again, flopping
on dog day concrete.

Chicago's Unhealthy Atmosphere

is blind from sleep
    and Gustav steps into
    the bathroom.

He reaches the sink,
begins because he can't find

the toilet. Because cold blooded
    porcelain softens his face.

In his dreams, the lamp
is a child begging change.

Worn clothes, teeth corrupt
    from nights on the street.

I don't have any change,
Gustav mumbles, returning

to bed. A cocoon of blankets
    and he sleeps quickly,
        dreams parading children,

mouths full of decaying teeth.

"Procession of the Dead"

Klimt's parting is a hiss.
        Exhaust of his body—

dry breath from
the waning shape pulled
        into the caravan.

His skin, left airing
beneath the city's sun.

His hair, left. Still damp
from hunching, bottom
of a stained tub.
                    Shivering
from patchwork anecdotes

babbling from a rusted spigot.

Government Magic

Soldiers chucked Fela's mother
from the third story before setting
Kalakuta on fire. They thought

no one was listening: igneous
crackling as it thaws, machete
cough in night's sediment. Birds

crooning baobobs pantomimed
after petrol. Kalakuta, reagent
of want. Birthmark from flame

so thick it still gnaws brick by brick.
One thousand soldiers side-stepped
Fela, all coral snake and antiphonic

feathers. The brush's narrative, tales
in twigs, fire ants, mosquito dream
songs were war paint that morning.

Some of his thirty wives were there,
even if "Anikulapo" means *one
who holds death in his pouch.*

Hypnosis and obeah end alike. *Álá*
seizing synapses and Fela, under
the same salmon colored skullcap.

Memento

As if on a normal day,
re-defining hours and minutes
comes snapshot simple,
like drinking from a fountain.
Forget the difficulty of learning:
water in the mouth, not up
the nose. Down the throat,
ignore the puddled shirt front.
Photo from the yearbook,
singling one extraordinary
stumble down the stairs
from the rest of the simple
ones. Simplicity is inane:
twenty-six muscle movements for
a mouthful of water to shimmy
from tongue to belly. A few
more to play the intro
to "Alabama," even if Coltrane
makes it seem involuntary.
On a normal day, it's possible
to drown in the shower.
Possible to remember
your first lover through
leftover perfume misted
on a telephone receiver.
Your best friend's admission—
Uncle molested her at knife
point—is a titanic day
in progress: *He didn't even
have his own shadow. Just
watery cologne and that knife.*

White Pages

Three years later and there are more Bennett, M.'s in the Indianapolis metropolitan phone book than there used to be. What was that street you lived on? I can't remember. It's 11:24 am, Wednesday; most respectable people are at work. I could call every listing, listen to the answering machine for the scrape of your voice. Like I did last time I lost your number. You were angry for a week: *You mean you don't have it memorized?* I didn't, but knew your curves like my favorite Lee Morgan sprint. I can still draw the trumpets in your lips upside down.

Peace and Soul

1. *It wasn't me, baby.*

Until I ratted him out, Mom's
suspicions were ethereal: Dad
and uncle, shim-bang hips shaped
by the Hustle. Mom thought
the afro-topped hot pants between
looked familiar, but Dad would
say *It's just dance, baby.* Things
changed when I named the girl
Diane, gave her character traits:
giver of cakes and candy Tuesdays,
owner of Lincoln Logs unsafe
for children. Don Cornelius' peace
and soul didn't stop me from naming
others for immunity from the wooden
spoon. Suzy, with the fight-starting
son. Jennifer, with a neighbor who
took me to the same movie house
twice a week. Jennifer's best friend,
Esmeralda, able to cut hair easy
on the scalp. My mother didn't confront.
She arranged her rendezvous:
part-time job altering clothing, needle
pricks hidden in dishes and soapy water.
Dad didn't find out until three years
later. We were on a plane to Indiana
without him, where *Soul Train* reruns
aired Sunday nights at eleven.

2. *Reruns*

I haven't watched *Soul Train* since Los Angeles,
scanning for my father's pat afro, perfect polyester
buttoned 1/3 up, exposing the Native American in him:

five chest hairs neatly greased to look like eight. It's
been longer since I spoke with the man himself. Today
I'm watching for my father's spindly dance, something

between a spider coughing and a man too cool for himself
tripping down the stairs. He hasn't been on the show
since '75, wanting to be like his pal Isaac Hayes, though

genealogy wouldn't allow goatee growth. Mom's stoicism
toward bald heads, her refusal of Issac's wedding invitation
kept them from becoming homemade twins. Calling Mom

possessive implies insecurity, but by that time, she knew
he was cheating. *Soul Train*, like a junkie dealing dope,
only made it easier. Dad signed his last letter "Peace and Soul,"

a few years before Don Cornelius retired. I wonder how Dad
jibes: probably retired, fixating on the tepid nature of beauty
in an oasis of geriatrics. Ivan Albright without epiphany: sixty

years old, Agent Orange orthopedically tucked away, hips too
arthritic for the Hustle, still good for the Robot. Dad's *Soul Train*
doesn't even exist as reruns anymore. Only on satellite,

some youngblood mush-mouthing "Peace and Soul" to end
each show. I can't afford satellite. I have to watch at Mom's
house: one more thing you understand when family is gone.

Vinyl

While marriage was difficult, the divorce
was simple. Dad packed, Mom watched.
Dad got the records, Mom got the kids:
three afroed half-and-halfs with no idea
of the goings on. That was Germany, after
Agent Orange helped color the apartment

with Mom's blood. After Mom rat-holed
enough money to leave. Divorce was just
the beginning: no need to mention sister,
waiting by the window like a storybook lover.
Or my daily evac of the school bus,
to be sure Mom would still be there when

I came home. What is worth mentioning
are the records. Before Dad and I loaded
the car with them, Mom put a dot of glue
on each one, vinyl gently returned to sleeve.
There was significance for her in two thousand
drops. Three tubes worth, if I remember right.

Visions of Max Roach

1.

1957, Max Roach rummaging
    through tom and cymbal arpeggios
for a momentary revolution

    of pitch. But in the real,
he's so old he only plays
    on holidays. Cymbal stutter

for Easter, snare celebration
    on Labor Day. I've never really
heard a Max Roach riff, any more

    than I thought I heard call
and response—shim-bang soloing
    tag-teamed with bass grumbling

only Mingus understands.
    Max's stick and wrist rim shots
are just static corralled on vinyl.

2.

    Today must be a holiday:
Max Roach at the Jazz Alley,
    an overpriced building, nothing

more than temporary cover
for rain-spent Seattle. A helper
tuned the set—a snare, two cymbals,

a bass drum—but Max looks lost.
Someone may as well have handed
him a whisk and a hammer instead

of sticks. Memory doesn't fade
necessarily, it just reorganizes.
As I remember it, there was no

confusion in Max, no dropped
drumsticks or embarrassed crowd.
But a man playing a tuba, brass

wrapped around him like a second
skin, yelling: *Do it, Max. Do it.*

Postlude

Music, all its squawks
and squeaks. Heart-beat
music, misery music:
I once believed nothing
was more singular
for a human than to turn
belly twists into song.
I have to make
an adjustment. I have
to revise: man's invention
is romance and without that,
he has jack. I apologize
for the oversight, but
as I sit, cave of flesh
where I once had a heart,
sounds seem less important.
Only half as harmonious
as before, sounds lapsed
in the vocal fold. But I can
still see shapes. More often
than not, I remember
the names of things.

N O T E S

The Devil's Garden is inside the Craters of the Moon National Monument, Oregon.

Ode to Eddie Hazel: a coffle is the metal binder used to connect a group of slaves at the necks to prevent them from running away.

Earth Will Seduce You is a line borrowed from Louise Glück's "The Sensual World."

Me in The Garden of Music: painting by Bob Thompson, 1960.

For What It's Worth is a derivative of Sujata Bhatt's poem "What is Worth Knowing."

Eight Positions Mistaken as Love is a contrafact of "The 32 Positions of Love" from *The Immaculate Conception* by Paul Eluard and André Breton.

Government Magic: Álá is light in the Spiritual sense of that which brings illumination or enlightenment.

Memento is based on the painting "Titanic Days" by René Magritte, 1928.

The Wind, Master Cherry, the Wind, Larissa Szporluk
North True South Bright, Dan Beachy-Quick
My Mojave, Donald Revell
Granted, Mary Szybist
Sails the Wind Left Behind, Alessandra Lynch
Sea Gate, Jocelyn Emerson
An Ordinary Day, Xue Di
The Captain Lands in Paradise, Sarah Manguso
Ladder Music, Ellen Doré Watson
Self and Simulacra, Liz Waldner
Live Feed, Tom Thompson
The Chime, Cort Day
Utopic, Claudia Keelan
Pity the Bathtub Its Forced Embrace of the Human Form,
  Matthea Harvey
Isthmus, Alice Jones
The Arrival of the Future, B.H. Fairchild
The Kingdom of the Subjunctive, Suzanne Wise
Camera Lyrica, Amy Newman
How I Got Lost So Close to Home, Amy Dryansky
Zero Gravity, Eric Gamalinda
Fire & Flower, Laura Kasischke
The Groundnote, Janet Kaplan
An Ark of Sorts, Celia Gilbert
The Way Out, Lisa Sewell
The Art of the Lathe, B.H. Fairchild
Generation, Sharon Kraus
Journey Fruit, Kinereth Gensler
We Live in Bodies, Ellen Doré Watson
Middle Kingdom, Adrienne Su
Heavy Grace, Robert Cording
Proofreading the Histories, Nora Mitchell
We Have Gone to the Beach, Cynthia Huntington
The Wanderer King, Theodore Deppe
Girl Hurt, E.J. Miller Laino

ALICE JAMES BOOKS has been publishing exclusively poetry since 1973. One of the few presses in the country that is run collectively, the cooperative selects manuscripts for publication through both regional and national annual competitions. New regional authors become active members of the cooperative, participating in the editorial decisions of the press. The press, which historically placed an emphasis on publishing women poets, was named for Alice James, sister of William and Henry, whose fine journal and gift for writing went unrecognized within her lifetime.

TYPESET AND DESIGNED BY MIKE BURTON

PRINTED BY THOMSON-SHORE